ONE DIRECTION!

By Fiona Davis

LEVEL 1

Written by: Fiona Davis
Publisher: Jacquie Bloese
Editor: Sarah Silver
Designer: Dawn Wilson
Picture research: Pupak Navabpour
Photo credits:
Cover: S. Jaye/Rex Features; brainmaster/iStockphoto.
Pages 4 & 5: F. Duval, M. Davis, T. Whitby, S. Wilson, J. Merritt, D. Hogan/Getty Images; Splash/Corbis; ultraforma/iStockphoto.
Pages 6 & 7: Agencia el Universal/Photoshot
Pages 9 - 11: D. Berehulak, X Factor, S. Wilson/Getty Images.
Pages 14 & 15: Beretta/Sims/Rex Features; F. Brown/Getty Images.
Pages 16 & 17: M. Kent, D. Hogan, S. Wilson/Getty Images.
Pages 18 & 19: J. Pellegrini, N. Galai/Getty Images.
Pages 20 & 21: D. Hogan, N. Barnard/Getty Images.
Pages 22 & 23: New York Daily News, I. Gavan/Getty Images.
Pages 24 & 25: New York Daily News, S. Wilson/Getty Images.
Pages 26 & 27: Zuma/Rex Features; J. Sato/Wire Image/Getty Images.
Pages 28 & 29: D. Hogan/Getty Images; Beretta/Sims/Rex Features.
Pages 30 & 31: D. Hogan, I. Gavan/Getty Images.
Pages 32 & 33: China Foto Press/Getty Images.
Pages 34 & 35: P. Hebert, P. Bergen/Redferns, M. Carr /Getty Images; egeeksen/iStockphoto.

Published by Scholastic Ltd. 2014

No part of this publication may be reproduced in whole or in part, or stored in a retrieval system, or transmitted in any form or by any means, electronic, mechanical, photocopying, recording or otherwise, without written permission of the publisher. For information regarding permission write to:

Mary Glasgow Magazines (Scholastic Ltd.)
Euston House
24 Eversholt Street
London NW1 1DB

All rights reserved

Printed in Singapore

CONTENTS

	PAGE
One Direction	**4–33**
People and places	4–5
On top of the world	6–7
Chapter 1: The X Factor Dream	8
Harry Styles	11
Chapter 2: 'The next big boy band'	13
Liam Payne	17
Chapter 3: 'The best fans'	18
Louis Tomlinson	21
Niall Horan	25
Chapter 4: On the road	26
Zayn Malik	31
Fact File	**34–35**
Self-Study Activities	**36–39**
New Words	**40**

PEOPLE AND PLACES

THIS IS ONE DIRECTION!

One Direction first sang together in 2010 on The X Factor. They are now one of the most famous pop bands on the world.

ZAYN MALIK was seventeen when he auditioned for X Factor.

NIALL HORAN always wanted to be a singer.

LIAM PAYNE started singing when he was six.

LOUIS TOMLINSON likes to write songs.

HARRY STYLES is the youngest member of the band.

THE X FACTOR JUDGES

The X Factor is a TV competition for new singers and bands. Simon Cowell is the most famous judge on The X Factor. Louis Walsh worked with famous UK boy bands Boyzone and Westlife. Nicole Scherzinger and Katy Perry are singers.

SIMON   NICOLE

LOUIS   KATY

PLACES

The O2 Arena in London where the band started their *Take Me Home* world tour in 2013.

The band have a lot of time in their tour bus. The boys sleep, eat and play computer games on the bus!

THE FANS

One Direction fans are called 'Directioners'. There are millions of Directioners all around the world.

On top of the world

Three number one albums in three years.

Take Me Home tour, Foro Sol Stadium, Mexico City: 50,000 fans each night.

Niall Horan @NiallOfficial
Mexico City! Thank you so much for having us! X

Harry Styles @Harry_Styles
It's the last show in Brisbane tonight. Thank you everyone who came. You were very loud. xx

Twelve million DVDs, albums and blu-rays sold in one year.

April 2013 Six shows at London's O2 – all sold out in minutes!

zaynmalik1D @zaynmalik
Thank you for everything, you truly are the best fans in the world. Love you all x

Louis Tomlinson @Louis_Tomlinson
Great show again today!! Loveeee.

Liam Payne @Real_Liam_Payne
Who's at the Seattle show tonight? … I am :)

Five young singers – over ten million Twitter followers each. But three years before, no one knew them …

CHAPTER 1
The X Factor dream

June, 2010. It was very early in the morning and Zayn Malik did not want to get up. He was very nervous but his mum pulled him out of bed. It was one of the most important days of his life. Zayn had an audition for The X Factor.

In Manchester, lots of singers waited for their chance to audition. Harry Styles was one of them. Harry was in a band with some friends from school. His dream was to be a famous singer.

'How old are you?' asked Simon Cowell when Harry walked out onto the stage.

'I'm 16,' answered Harry.

The judges liked Harry's song, but Louis Walsh said 'no'. 'I think you're so young,' he said.

'I like you, Harry,' said Nicole Scherzinger. 'I'm going to say 'yes.' Harry was through to Bootcamp!

When Zayn walked out onto the stage, he was still very nervous. There were a lot of people there and the judges sat at the front.

'What are you going to sing?' asked Simon.

Zayn sang Mario's 'Let Me Love You.' He only sang part of the song before the judges stopped him. The three judges said 'yes'! He was through to Bootcamp too.

Louis Tomlinson was one of the last singers to audition in Manchester. Louis had two hours sleep the night before the audition. He was also very nervous and his singing wasn't very strong. But it was enough for the judges. They all said 'yes'.

In Dublin, Niall Horan enjoyed singing in front of everyone, but the judges weren't all happy.

Have you got the X Factor?

The X Factor is one of the UK's favourite TV shows. The live TV shows run from August to December. But the competition starts long before that ...

AUDITIONS
First the contestants audition for the TV company. The TV company then chooses contestants to sing in front of the judges. Singers can go to Bootcamp if most of the judges say 'yes'.

BOOTCAMP
At Bootcamp the contestants are put into four different groups: boys, girls, bands and singers over 25. They all practise different songs and learn to dance. The best contestants go through to the judges' houses.

THE JUDGES' HOUSES
One judge works with each group. The contestants live and practise together for one week. At the end of the week, the judge chooses the contestants for the live TV shows.

LIVE SHOWS
There is a live show every Saturday. People in the UK choose the best singers. The winner of the competition has a recording contract with Simon Cowell's music company.

Thousands of people wait to audition for The X Factor

"You have got the X Factor"
=
There's something special about you.

What do these words mean? You can use a dictionary.
live   contestant   company   group   recording contract

'You came with the wrong song,' said Simon. But he and Louis Walsh liked the teenager from Ireland. The third judge said 'no'. Now Niall needed a 'yes' from judge, Katy Perry. Katy almost said 'no', but …

'Give him a chance!' said Louis.

'Of course, you're in!' said Katy.

Liam Payne first auditioned for The X Factor when he was fourteen. He was already a good singer, but Simon wanted him to stay at school. Now Liam was back at The X Factor auditions in Birmingham. Liam sang a very famous song, 'Cry Me A River'. Everyone loved it and Simon too! Liam was very happy. 'I can't stop smiling!' he laughed.

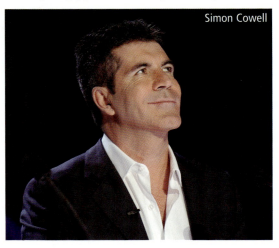

Simon Cowell

This was just the start of the competition. Bootcamp was next. There were 211 singers and bands at Bootcamp but only 32 places in the next part of the competition. There were singing classes and a dance class too.

For Zayn, the dance class was terrible. He didn't want to dance in front of other people. But Simon Cowell found him backstage.

HARRY

BORN: 1st February 1994

HOME TOWN: Harry comes from Holmes Chapel in the north-west of England.

FAMILY: Harry has one older sister.

WHEN HE WAS YOUNG: At high school Harry started singing with a band, called White Eskimo. They won a competition together.

LIKES: Harry likes to take photos and often puts them on Instagram.

HARRY FACTS:

★ Harry says is: 'Work hard, play hard, be kind.'

★ Harry had a Saturday job in a baker's shop for two and a half years.

ON GIRLS: Harry likes girls with nice eyes. For Harry it's important to have a laugh together.

FAVOURITES: Harry's favourite band is Coldplay. His favourite video game is FIFA.

TWITTER: @harry_styles

> What do these words mean?
> You can use a dictionary.
> **born   north-west   baker**

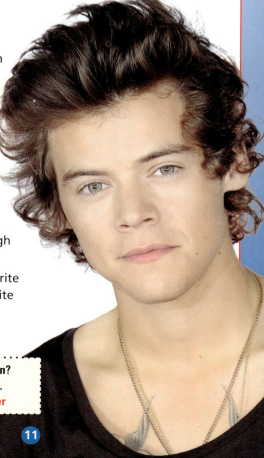

'Why aren't you out there?' he asked.

'I can't dance!' said Zayn.

Simon wanted everyone to dance so Zayn decided to try. He went out to the front of the stage.

At the end of Bootcamp, the judges had to choose the best singers. They read out the names of the winners. Not one of the five 1D boys was through. They were all very sad. Liam talked to the cameras, 'I just don't want to go home,' he said.

But then the judges called some of the singers back. For the first time, Harry, Liam, Louis, Niall and Zayn were together on stage.

'We've decided to put you through as a band,' said Simon.

The boys were very excited. Now they had a second chance!

1D WORDS

'From the worst feeling in my life to the best!'
Harry Styles at the end of Bootcamp.

CHAPTER 2
'The next big boy band'

The five boys were now a boy band. They had one week before the next part of the competition. The boys decided to go to Harry's house for that week.

For all the boys, it was important to be friends. They played football and they sang songs around the fire. They talked about their dreams for their new band. They wanted to have fun. They didn't want to all wear the same clothes and they didn't want to dance! They didn't want to be like other boy bands.

1D FACT Everyone in the band wanted the same things so Harry thought of the name: One Direction.

The next part of The X Factor was at the judges' houses. The boys went to Marbella in Spain with Simon Cowell. They had a lot of fun and went to the beach a lot! But they also worked hard. There were eight bands in Marbella. Simon Cowell had to choose only three.

The boys' last song was Natalie Imbruglia's 'Torn'. They loved singing together but Simon knew they were nervous. He liked One Direction, but the boys were very young. They waited all day to hear 'yes' or 'no'.

'It's only one word that can change your life,' said Harry. The wait was terrible, but then they heard from Simon.

'You're through!' he said.

'We were so happy,' remembered Liam later. 'We all went in the swimming pool with our clothes on!'

One Direction outside The X Factor

The boys went back to London for the X Factor TV shows. They lived together in a big room in the X Factor house, and there were clothes all over the floor! By now they were best friends and they enjoyed every minute of the competition! There were lots of photos, lots of people to meet and lots of parties!

But the boys also worked long hours every day. They got up early for singing classes. They listened to the judges. Every week they sang better and better and every week they had more and more fans.

There were ten weeks of live TV shows. The last people in the competition were Matt Cardle, Rebecca Ferguson and the new band, One Direction!

In week ten the boys went to their home towns. There were lots of screaming fans in every town!

The X Factor – the best bits

WEEK 1
One Direction start their competition by singing a Coldplay song, 'Viva La Vida'.

WEEK 2
Harry doesn't feel well because he is so nervous. But the other boys look after him and they sing well. Simon Cowell tells them, 'You are the most exciting pop band in the country today.'

WEEK 3
The boys sing 'Nobody knows'. Louis Walsh tells them they are the next big boy band.

WEEK 6
One Direction meet the Harry Potter star, Daniel Radcliffe. Daniel Radcliffe is a fan!

WEEK 7
One Direction sing The Beatles' song, 'All You Need Is Love'.

WEEK 8
The band sings Joe Cocker's 'You Are So Beautiful.' The song is difficult to sing and the boys sing very well. The judges love it! But it is difficult to hear the judges – the fans are screaming so loudly!

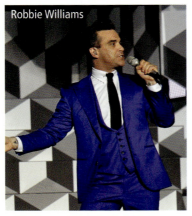
Robbie Williams

Back on the TV show, the band sang with their favourite singer, Robbie Williams, from the boy band Take That.

Many people wanted One Direction to win The X Factor. They were also Simon Cowell's favourite. After their last song, they waited nervously on stage with Simon. But to everyone's surprise, the boys came third. The boys were very sad. Was this the end of their dream? But there was still hope for their fans. Zayn told them, 'This isn't the last of One Direction!'.

One Direction with Simon Cowell on The X Factor

All about...

LIAM

BORN: 29th August 1993

HOME TOWN: Liam comes from Wolverhampton, a city in the middle of England.

FAMILY: He has two sisters.

WHEN HE WAS YOUNG: Liam started singing when he was about six years old. He liked singing in front of people. His favourite song was 'Angels' by Robbie Williams.

LIKES: Liam loves sport. When he was younger he did boxing. He's also a football fan.

LIAM FACTS:
★ He loves the Toy Story films.
★ His favourite actor is Johnny Depp.
★ In Australia, he learned to surf with Louis.
★ In 2013, Liam started dating Sophie Smith. She and Liam went to college together.

FAVOURITE 1D SONG: He loves singing 'C'mon C'mon'. The fans love the song too and sing it back!

TWITTER: @real_liam_payne

What do these words mean? You can use a dictionary.
born   boxing   actor   surf   college

CHAPTER 3
'The best fans'

After The X Factor, fans wanted to hear more songs from 1D. The fans used Twitter and Tumblr to talk about the band. They put the band's X Factor songs on YouTube. Soon One Direction had fans all over the world. Some fans tweeted about the band all the time. The boys tweeted back.

1D WORDS   'We have the best fans in the world!' *Niall Horan*

One Direction only came third in The X Factor, but Simon Cowell wanted to make an album with them. They started recording the album in January 2011. The band's first song was 'What Makes You Beautiful'. It came out in the UK in September 2011 and went to number one on the same day. The fans loved it!

One Direction with their first album *Up All Night*

The album *Up All Night* came out in November. The songs were fun and talked about young love. Also on the album were the hits 'Gotta Be You' and 'One Thing'.

1D FACT Songwriter Savan Kotecha gave singing classes on The X Factor and also wrote some of One Direction's biggest hits. With songwriters Rami Yakoub and Carl Falk, Kotecha wrote '*What Makes You Beautiful*', '*One Thing*' and '*Live While We're Young*'.

One Direction also had thousands of young fans in the US. Sixteen-year-old Canadian singer, Justin Bieber, was already a hit with teenagers in the US, but there were not many boy bands at that time.

Up All Night came out in the US in March 2012. The album went to number one on the same day. The band went to New York and played on *The Today Show**. More than 15,000 fans came to see them. Many fans waited outside for two or three days.

Fans waiting to see One Direction in New York

* *The Today Show* is a morning TV show in the US.

Suddenly, the five boys from Britain were one of the most famous bands in the world. But for the boys it was about more than this. They loved singing and they loved their fans. But perhaps the most important thing to them was the other 1D boys. The five boys were good friends from the start. But now they lived and worked together. They went everywhere together. They were famous together.

1D WORDS

'I always wanted a little brother. Now I've got four of them.' *Liam Payne*

At the end of 2011 the band started their *Up All Night* tour. They played sixty concerts around the UK and Ireland, North America, Australia and New Zealand. In November 2012 their second album, *Take Me Home*, was number one in 37 countries.

All about... LOUIS

BORN: 24th December 1991

HOME TOWN: Louis comes from Doncaster. Doncaster is a city in Yorkshire, in the north of England.

FAMILY: He has five half-sisters.

WHEN HE WAS YOUNG: When he was younger, Louis wanted to be an actor. When he was fourteen, he sang in a band for a short time and loved it.

LIKES: Louis loves football. He sometimes plays for the football team in Doncaster. Louis also loves tweeting – usually about football!

LOUIS FACTS:
★ He is the oldest singer in the band.
★ The other boys say that Louis is very messy on tour!

ON GIRLS: Louis is a funny guy. It's important for Louis that his girlfriend is funny too, and has a good smile.

FAVOURITE SONG: His favourite song is 'Look After You' by The Fray.

TWITTER: @louis_tomlinson

> **What do these words mean?**
> **You can use a dictionary.**
> born   half-sister   actor   messy

On December the 3rd 2012, One Direction played Madison Square Garden in New York. In the US, Madison Square Garden is one of the most famous places for bands to play. The New York concert was a sell-out. For the boys it was one of their best concerts.

The boys were nervous before the concert. Was it because there were 20,000 people at the concert? No, it was because the boys' families were there! It was a special time for the boys' families and friends.

Louis went to Bootcamp in July 2010. He didn't go home again for two and a half years. Harry's mum says that sixteen-year-old Harry left home on the day of his X Factor audition. For all the boys, this is the sad thing about their success. When the boys are home, they spend time with friends and family and this is important to them. Zayn has three sisters and they come to as many concerts as they can.

One Direction on stage at Madison Square Garden

One Direction are famous across the world. It's thanks to their fans and the boys never forget this. Louis says that 1D is teamwork between the five singers and their fans.

Directioners want to know everything about the boys. When the band goes places, they are always waiting. The boys are all good-looking and every fan has their favourite. But for the fans, it is about more than looks. The boys are very successful, but they are still normal guys. They are young and they have fun. Directioners love them for this.

Words from Directioners:

'Every time I see them it puts a smile on my face.'

'They are real and aren't afraid to be themselves.'

'They remember who they are and where they're from.'

'I LOVE ONE DIRECTION!! THEY ARE MY LIFE!! NEVER CHANGE!! ... MY DREAM IS TO MEET THEM!!!!!'

There were also some very special fans at the Madison Square Garden concert. The boys wanted to meet some of their fans so they started 'Bring Me to 1D'. Fans took part in lots of competitions. They made books and videos and took photos. The boys gave golden tickets to the winners. The winners came from forty different countries. They met the boys and there was a small concert just for them.

Directioners at the concert in Madison Square Garden

In February 2013 One Direction went to Ghana in Africa with Comic Relief. It changed their lives. Comic Relief gives money to the poor people of the world. The boys saw life for some of the people in Africa. They saw a lot of children in hospital and they were very sad. But the boys also loved the people. Life was very hard, but the people were often happy.

1D FACT One Direction recorded 'ced_One Way Or Another_' for Comic Relief. The song made more than two million pounds for people in Africa.

NIALL

BORN: 13th September 1993

HOME TOWN: Niall's home town is Mullingar. Mullingar is a town in the centre of Ireland.

FAMILY: He has one brother.

WHEN HE WAS YOUNG: At school Niall wanted to be a singer. He wrote this on his desk.

LIKES: Niall likes playing football and golf.

NIALL FACTS:

★ Niall started playing guitar when he was eleven.

★ He was always late for school.

FAVOURITES: Niall's favourite film is Grease.

His favourite boybands are 'N Sync, Backstreet Boys and, of course, 1D!

ON GIRLS: Niall meets lots of fans but he still feels nervous if he likes a girl!

TWITTER: @NiallOfficial

> What do these words mean?
> You can use a dictionary.
> **born   golf**

CHAPTER 4
On the road

In 2013 there were more chances for Directioners to see their favourite band. The *Take Me Home* world tour started at the O2 arena in London in February 2013 and finished with two concerts in Japan in November. One Direction sang at 134 concerts on tour and most concerts sold out in minutes.

1D FACT Singer Ed Sheeran wrote 'Little Things', one of 1D's favourite songs. It is a love song and sometimes the boys cry when they sing it on stage!

Directioners waited in line for many hours before the start of a show. The boys opened with 'Up All Night'. The stage was fantastic. Behind the band were films of cities, comic books and video games. The boys had no special

The boys having a laugh on stage

1D on tour

On tour, it's not just about the concerts. In Harry's words, he likes being with his four friends, 'going to cool places, meeting lots of nice people and having a laugh'.

The boys are flying or on the road a lot of the time. The boys enjoy their tour bus. They can watch films, play video games and have time to phone home.

The boys are sometimes very tired. One Direction recorded their third album on the *Take Me Home* tour. They played concerts at night and then got up early to go to the recording studio.

The crew is their family on tour and their 'dad' is tour manager, Paul Higgins. The boys and the crew have a lot of fun together. The boys often have a laugh with the crew. A few minutes before the start of a concert the boys are often running around and fighting with the crew. But when the music starts, the band is always ready.

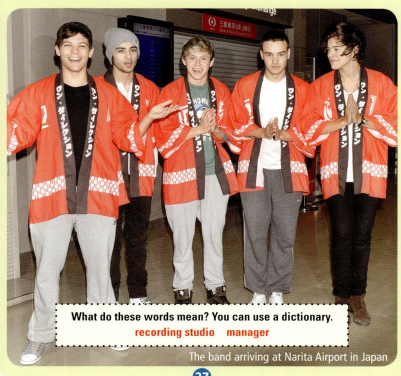

What do these words mean? You can use a dictionary.
recording studio   manager

The band arriving at Narita Airport in Japan

dance moves or special clothes. They did their own funny dance moves. The boys just enjoyed singing and having fun together. Between songs the boys talked and answered tweets from the fans. The fans felt part of the show.

1D FACT When the video for 'Best Song Ever' came out, 12.3 million people watched it in the first twenty-four hours.

Cameras follow One Direction all the time, but for the *Take Me Home* tour, the cameras came backstage too. American director, Morgan Spurlock, wanted to make a film about the band. He filmed their lives for six months of the tour – onstage and backstage.

Onstage the boys sang their hits and also their new song 'Best Song Ever'. Backstage the boys laughed at their dancing, ran away from the crew and met their fans. Morgan loved working with the boys. He liked them from the start. In their first meeting they all had a food fight!

Harry with director Morgan Spurlock before the opening of the film *This Is Us*

1D – the funny bits

⭐ The night before a concert in Amsterdam, the band tweeted for everyone to wear orange. The next day, everyone at the concert had orange clothes – and the band too.

⭐ On tour, Harry and Liam dressed up as old people and walked around the streets. It was a surprise for everyone when they suddenly ran away very fast!

⭐ Louis once said 'I like girls who eat carrots.' Now fans often give him carrots!

⭐ At big concerts, there are often carts backstage. The boys love to drive them. The crew have to run after them!

⭐ It's hard to have a good night's sleep on tour. Louis wakes the others up – by throwing water over them! There are also lots of food fights!

> **What do these words mean? You can use a dictionary.**
> dress up   carrot   cart   throw

This Is Us film premiere in London

The film, *This Is Us*, was a hit with the fans. The boys loved the opening night. On their way to the première*, they tweeted fans. 'Can't wait to see ya all' (Niall) 'Hereee weeee goooo!!!!!' (Liam)

The third album *Midnight Memories* came out after the tour. This album had a different sound to it. Niall played guitar. Louis and Liam helped write many of the songs with American songwriter Julian Bunetta. The words of the songs meant a lot to them.

1D FACT November the 23rd, 2013 was 1D Day. The boys were live on YouTube for seven hours!

* *première* = opening night of a film

All about... ZAYN

BORN: 12th January 1993

HOME TOWN: Zayn's home town is Bradford, Yorkshire. Yorkshire is in the north of England.

FAMILY: He has three sisters. His father is from Pakistan. His mother is English.

WHEN HE WAS YOUNG: Zayn always loved singing. When he was twelve, he went to drama school.

LIKES: Zayn loves drawing. He has a special room in his house for drawing. He draws on the walls too!

ZAYN FACTS

★ Zayn bought his family a new house.

★ He always wears two pairs of socks!

★ In 2013, Zayn got engaged to Perrie Edwards from Little Mix. Little Mix won The X Factor in 2011.

FAVOURITE 1D SONGS: He likes singing '*Tell Me A Lie*' and '*More Than This*' on stage.

TWITTER: @zaynmalik

What do these words mean? You can use a dictionary.
born   north   drama   pair   get engaged

In three years the boys' lives changed so much. On 22nd July 2013, three years after the start of Bootcamp, Harry Styles tweeted to the fans: 'Thank you so much for everything. We are so lucky to have you. You keep making it more and more fun.'

In November of that year, the boys went back on The X Factor and sang 'Story Of My Life'. The boys took turns to sing and were not at all nervous!

The story of One Direction is about music, dreams, hard work, fans and most important of all, five friends. How does Louis want people to think of One Direction? 'They just had fun, and they're just normal guys, but terrible, terrible dancers!'

1D WORDS

'A dream is only a dream … until you decide to make it real.' *Harry Styles*

One Direction in Japan

FACT FILE

BEHIND THE BAND

Pop stars work hard to be famous, but they can't do it alone. They work with lots of different people. Read on to find out about some of the people behind today's music stars.

Max won an award for best songwriter in 2013

THE SONGWRITER

All good singers need a good song. And behind every hit there is a great songwriter. Max Martin from Sweden is one of the most successful songwriters today. He has more than 35 hit songs and many awards. Max writes songs for Katy Perry, Taio Cruz, Usher and more. Songwriters often work in small teams with the singer and also produce the album.

What other jobs are there in music? Can you find out?

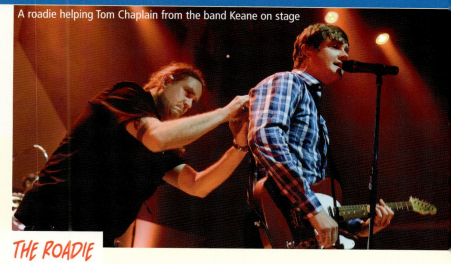
A roadie helping Tom Chaplain from the band Keane on stage

THE ROADIE

Musicians and singers make most of their money on tour. And the roadies go with them. Roadies work on the lights and the sound. They also look after the instruments so roadies are often musicians too.

A good roadie loves the stage, but doesn't want to be on it! But some musicians start as roadies. Krist Novoselic was a roadie before starting the band Nirvana with Kurt Cobain.

Floria Sigismondi

THE VIDEO DIRECTOR

The music video is very important to the success of a record. Video directors get their first ideas just by listening to the song.

Floria Sigismondi is a photographer and video director. Her video for Justin Timberlake's 'Mirrors' was MTV's best music video in 2013. There is not always a lot of money for a music video, but Floria says this is not always important. With little money, directors are sometimes more creative.

What do these words mean? You can use a dictionary.

award   produce   musician   instrument   director   creative

SELF-STUDY ACTIVITIES

CHAPTER 1

Before you read
You can use your dictionary.

1 Answer these questions.
   a) Can you name a famous **singer**?
   b) What **song** does he or she sing?
   c) Do you have an **album** by this singer?

2 Complete the sentences about The X Factor with these words.
   audition   chance   competition   fans   judges   tour   winner
   a) Do you want to be a singer? The X Factor can give you the ....
   b) The X Factor is a singing ....
   c) Singers .... in front of three or four ....
   d) The .... of the competition makes an album.
   e) They play at concerts and .... come to see them.
   f) Sometimes they go on .... around the country.

3 Look at 'People and places' on pages 4–5. Are these people singers, X Factor judges or both? Write S, J or B.
   a) Simon Cowell ☐
   b) Zayn Malik ☐
   c) Nicole Scherzinger ☐
   d) Louis Tomlinson ☐
   e) Louis Walsh ☐

After you read

4 Choose the correct word(s).
   a) *Zayn Malik / Harry Styles* sang in a band at school.
   b) Louis auditioned for The X Factor in *Birmingham / Manchester*.
   c) *All / Some* of the judges said 'yes' to Niall Horan.
   d) Liam had his first X Factor audition when he was *fourteen / sixteen*.
   e) After the auditions, the boys went to *Bootcamp / the live TV shows*.
   f) *The judges / people in the UK* choose the winner of The X Factor.

CHAPTER 2

Before you read

5 All these places are important in Chapter 2. Can you guess why?
Harry's house   Marbella, Spain   London
Now read and check.

After you read

6 Answer these questions.
   a) Who thought of the name One Direction?
   b) Which judge put 1D through to the live shows?
   c) What Beatles song did 1D sing in the X Factor competition?
   d) What places did the boys visit before their last X Factor show?

7 Find and correct the mistakes in these sentences.
   a) One Direction wanted to be like other boy bands.
   b) In London, each boy had their own room.
   c) Fans hated One Direction from the start.
   d) Simon Cowell wanted Take That to win The X Factor.
   e) One Direction won The X Factor.

8 Who says these things?
   Simon Cowell   Zayn Malik   Liam Payne   Harry Styles   Louis Walsh
   a) 'It's only one word that can change your life!'
   b) 'You're through!'
   c) 'We were so happy!'
   d) 'You are the next big boy band.'
   e) 'This isn't the last of One Direction!'

9 Tick the facts which are true about Liam.
   a) His birthday is in August.   ☐
   b) His favourite actor is Johnny Depp.   ☐
   c) His favourite band is Coldplay.   ☐
   d) He loves football.   ☐
   e) He has one sister.   ☐

The other facts are about a different 1D singer. Who is it?

SELF-STUDY ACTIVITIES

CHAPTER 3

Before you read

10 Complete the sentences with these words.

concert   hit   normal   record   sell-out   successful

  a) A very popular song is a ....
  b) Singers .... albums of songs.
  c) A .... band has thousands of fans.
  d) A .... is a .... when you can't buy more tickets.
  e) .... things are things that you do or see usually.

After you read

11 Match the titles with their descriptions.
  a) Up All Night   i) a competition
  b) Take Me Home   ii) the first album and tour
  c) Look After You   iii) the first hit
  d) Bring Me to 1D   iv) Louis Tomlinson's favourite song
  e) What Makes You Beautiful v) the second album and tour

12 Put these events in order.
  a) 1D went to Ghana.
  b) Their first song came out.
  c) They started recording their first album.
  d) Their first album came out in the US.
  e) The X Factor finished.

13 Complete these sentences about 1D fans.

forget   know   love   put   waited

  a) After The X Factor, fans .... the band's songs on YouTube.
  b) The band are all 'normal guys' and the fans .... this.
  c) The fans want to .... everything about the band.
  d) Fans .... outside The Today Show for two or three days.
  e) One Direction never .... their fans!

14 Why are these important in the story of One Direction?
    Simon Cowell   Savan Kotecha   Madison Square Garden   Twitter

CHAPTER 4

Before you read
15 Do you have a favourite singer in One Direction? Why is he your favourite?

After you read
16 Which of these do One Direction do? Tick the boxes.
   a) answer tweets from fans ☐
   b) have fun together ☐
   c) learn special dance moves ☐
   d) meet lots of people ☐
   e) stay at home all day ☐

17 Are these sentences true or false? Correct the false sentences.
   a) The *Take Me Home* tour started in the US.
   b) The boys' stage show was boring.
   c) Morgan Spurlock is a director.
   d) Zayn played guitar on the new album *Midnight Memories*.
   e) The band went back on The X Factor in November 2013.

18 Choose the correct word.
   a) The fans in Amsterdam wore *green / orange*.
   b) The boys have lots of *book / food* fights.
   c) The boys *drive carts / ride bikes* backstage.
   d) Louis wakes the others up by throwing *carrots / water* over them.

19 Tick the facts which are true about Zayn.
   a) He was born in Ireland. ☐
   b) He went to drama school. ☐
   c) He plays guitar. ☐
   d) He draws in his free time. ☐
   e) He likes socks. ☐

The other facts are about a different 1D singer. Who is it?

20 What do you think? One Direction are a very successful boy band. Can you think of three reasons for this?

NEW WORDS

What do these words mean?

album (n) ....

audition (n&v) ....

chance (n) ....

competition (n) ....

concert (n) ....

crew (n) ....

fan (n) ....

fight (n) ....

hit (n) ....

judge (n) ....

nervous (adj) ....

normal (adj) ....

record (v) ....

sang (v, past) .... / singing (n) .... /
   song (n) ....

scream (v) ....

sell-out (n) .... / sold out (v) ....

stage (n) .... / backstage (n) .... /
   onstage (n) ....

success (n) .... / successful (adj) ....

(on) tour (n) ....

win (v) .... / winner (n) ....